DAD'S LITTLE KING

BY

DONNA WEBERNICK

DAD'S LITTLE KING

BY
DONNA WEBERNICK

All graphics were taken from Canva and included in my design.

Dear Reader,
I wrote this book for my friend Bro. Claude and Sis. Lillian Prince. It is based on a true story about their dog, King. Thank you for your purchase.

Many Blessings,

Donna Webernick

Dad adored his daughter's puppy, King, and always wanted her fur baby to come home with him.

He loves playing with King so much that she gave King to her dad as a birthday gift.

"Dad was thrilled to have his furry
baby come live with him."

They go on walks together. Dad
sings him a good morning song
every morning while they walk.

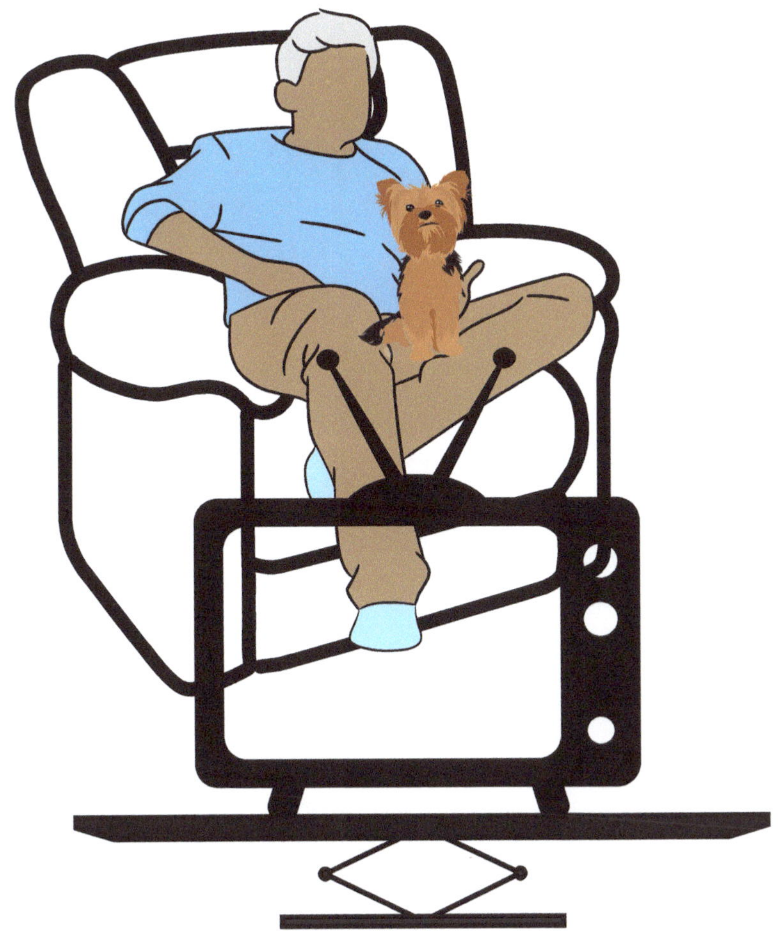

"They watch TV together."

"Sometimes, they take naps together."

Dad took King to the veterinarian to have his nails trimmed.

King was terrified, but Dad embraced him and reassured him, "You'll be okay, little buddy."

After the vet visit, Dad took King
home and gave him a treat.

"King was so happy that he wagged
his tail and jumped up and down."

After having his snack, he went into
his kennel to lie down for a nap.

"While King was sleeping, Dad went
outside to mow the yard."

"When King woke up from his nap,
he wondered where his dad had
gone."

He started barking. Mom told King, "Stop barking! Dad will be back soon."

Mom let King out of his kennel to play with his ball.

When Dad came into the house
from mowing, King was excited to
see him. So, Dad said," Let's go for a
walk King."

King wandered from yard to yard, sniffing everything. He was thrilled to be with his dad and to be outdoors.

After their walk, Mom gave King a
bath.

After bathing, King returned to his
Kennel to play with his toys.

Dad was engrossed in his game
shows on TV and missed his little
buddy sitting on his lap.

"Dad yelled to King,
'Come watch TV with me, little
buddy.'"

King comes running and jumps onto
Dad's lap.

"Both of them were happy, and
Mom was laughing."

When it was time for bed, Dad said, "King, it is time to go night, night, little buddy; I will see you in the morning."

King went into his kennel and fell
fast asleep.